poetic license / poetic justice

Also by Allan Douglass Coleman

Like Father Like Son (Staten Island, NY: Villa Florentine Press, 2007, with Earl M. Coleman)

spine (Borgå, Finland: minipress, 2000, with Nina Sederholm)

Confirmation (Staten Island, NY: ADCO Enterprises, 1975; second edition, 1982)

Carbon Copy (Staten Island, NY: ADCO Enterprises, 1973)

Writing as A. D. Coleman

Depth of Field: Essays on Photography, Mass Media and Lens Culture (Albuquerque: University of New Mexico Press, 1998)

The Digital Evolution: Photography in the Electronic Age, Essays, Lectures and Interviews 1967-1998 (Munich: Nazraeli Press, 1998)

Tarnished Silver: After the Photo Boom, Essays on Photography and Related Matters, 1979-1989 (New York: Midmarch Arts Press, 1996)

*Critical Focus: Photography in the International Image Community (*Munich: Nazraeli Press, 1995)

Looking at Photographs: Animals (San Francisco: Chronicle Books, 1995)

The Photography A-V Program Directory (New York: PMI, Inc., 1980); co-authored with Douglas Sheer and Patricia Grantz

Light Readings: A Photography Critic's Writings, 1968-1978 (New York: Oxford University Press, 1979; Galaxy Books paperback, 1982; second edition, University of New Mexico Press, 1998)

Lee/Model/Parks/Samaras/Turner: Five Interviews Before the Fact (Boston: Photographic Resource Center, 1979; second edition, 1997)

The Grotesque in Photography: A Critical Survey (New York: Ridge Press/ Summit Books, 1977)

About previous works by the author

"Coleman has been one of the most assiduous, energetic and intelligent critics of photography during this decade of expansion, and also at times one of the most opinionated and infuriating." — Hilton Kramer, *New York Times*

"He is a lucid thinker and an elegant writer. ... In praise, Coleman's prose is transcendent; in reproof, he does not mince words." — Margarett Loke, *ARTnews*

"His essays serve as a reality check, even a null set, for those of us in museums and universities." — Rod Slemmons, *Blackflash* (Canada)

"Coleman is an intelligent, well-informed and often maliciously witty observer. ... [I]t is never less than a pleasure even to disagree with the erudite Mr. Coleman." — John Stathatos, *European Photography* (Germany)

"Coleman's approach to understanding photographs rests first and foremost on understanding how photographs are made, especially on the decisions that lead to interesting visual statements." — Vince Leo, *Afterimage*

"There are no sacred cows for Coleman, and he takes no prisoners. He is willing to hold all the individuals and institutions of the art world up to the same high standards of truth and morality." — Joseph Flack Weiler, *Print World*

"[N]one would deny that as this country's first and foremost photo critic [Coleman] has made a singular contribution to the field, broadening both the definition and discussion of photography." — Taylor Holliday, *The Wall Street Journal*

"Coleman's discussion of the impact of technology on traditional photography serves as a brilliant ... record of how new electronic tools have permeated our lives." — Daniel Carter, *Wired*

"Coleman's greatest asset ... is his ability to write with precision, clarity and even humour. ... Rarely does a critic write so well." — Gary Crighton, *British Journal of Photography*

"Coleman's writing ... is informative and unpretentious — a rare combination in art criticism of any kind." — Eric Lorberer, *Rain Taxi: Review of Books*

"Coleman is a superbly articulate art critic specializing in photography." — *Publishers' Weekly*

"Coleman ... might be considered either as a transitional figure between modernism and postmodernism or as the first postmodernist critic [in photography]." — Joel Eisinger, *Trace & Transformation: American Criticism of Photography in the Modernist Period*

"I've long admired your work and political honesty — wish we had more people like you in the U.K." — Jo Spence, letter to the author, 1991

"poetic license / poetic justice" © copyright 2006 by Allan D. Coleman. All other contents by Coleman © copyright 2020by Allan D. Coleman. All rights reserved. By permission of the author & Image/World Syndication Services, imageworld@nearbycafe.com.

Introduction and book design by © copyright 2020 by BARBARA ROSENTHAL.

Charles Bernstein's portion of the email exchange with Coleman © copyright 2014 by Charles Bernstein.

Picture credits:
This page (L-R): Isidor Fankuchen, Earl Coleman, and Wallace Waterfall converse while looking at a book Coleman is holding, ca. 1960. Photographer unknown. American Institute of Physics Emilio Segrè Visual Archives, Physics Today Collection.
P. 36: Portrait of Frances Coleman, ca. 1960, photographer unknown.
P. 38: Portrait of Earl Coleman, ca. 1960, Fabian Bachrach (detail).
P. 42: Portrait of Allan D. Coleman, ca. 1960, Rappoport Studios, NYC, 1960.
P. 43: eMediaLoft.org, Interior Shot, Night, 2014, photographer, Bill Creston.
Back cover: Portrait of Allan Coleman, 2018, © copyright 2018 by Harris Fogel.

Washington Street Press, 2020
WASHINGTON STREET PRESS is an imprint of eMediaLoft.org, NYC
washingtonstreetpress.com
eMediaLoft.org
ISBN: 978-0-9989004-3-8

poetic license / poetic justice

a footnote to "the london march" by david antin

with a commentary by charles bernstein

Allan Douglass Coleman

WASHINGTON STREET PRESS, NYC

Table of Contents

Publisher's Introduction .... p. 11

poetic license / poetic justice .... p. 13

Author's email exchange with Charles Bernstein .... p. 32

Obituaries for Author's Parents

        Frances Allan Coleman .... p. 38

        Earl Maxwell Coleman .... p. 40

Author's Afterword and Acknowledgements .... p. 42

About the Author .... p. 44

About the Press .... p. 45

Introduction

This book by Allan Douglass Coleman inaugurates the imprint WASHINGTON STREET PRESS. It does so because the author conducts readers toward ideal visions via real experience along a path beaconed by unusual ideas or artifacts or media. In this case, that was "the london march," a typewriter-fonted textwork by David Antin, on which Coleman hereby bitingly riffs.

At dinner in our loft one night, Allan was casually talking about Antin's textwork, and poetic license / poetic justice, his own writings about Antin's, the subject being Consultants Bureau, Inc., the Coleman family publishing house, where both had been employed. Another guest, Charles Bernstein, after reading the manuscript, emailed his thoughts. Allan obtained Bernstein's permission to include their email string, and thus our invitation to Allan to publish was even further reinforced!

As the project moved forward, it became evident that the owners of that family publishing company, the author's parents, to whom this book is dedicated, who figure prominently in Antin's piece and therefore become central in Coleman's, might warrant additional presence here. So we included the obituaries he had written of them both.

I've known Allan Coleman since 1981, when introduced to him as A. D. Coleman by Alex Harsley at the Fourth Street Photo Gallery. My admiration for him as an "ethicatarian" — my sobriquet for his piercing regard for righteousness and his struggle to form clear communication of it to others — has made poetic license / poetic justice the ideal first title on our booklist.

BARBARA ROSENTHAL
Publisher

Just keep talking, like they say, and with luck and genius maybe you'll get to be like extraordinary David Antin. Not only was he there, wherever — which is a very large place indeed — but he can tell you just what happened.

— Robert Creeley

poetic license/poetic justice
a footnote to
"the london march" (1968) by david antin

(for my parents, earl and frances coleman)

my father makes a personal appearance in a
somewhat famous poem by david antin or to put
a finer point on it david antin sketched out on
paper & then talked & taperecorded & transcribed
& published a section about my father in one of
his "talking" poems

no this isnt some nabokovian pale fire moment
nor an equivalent to art critic douglas crimp
deciding & declaring that a portion of a certain
piece of postmodernist architecture was about
him its actually my father clearly identifiable
though he isnt named & this section of the antin
poem describes an episode i lived through in
my early teens so i can verify it personally
my father vouches for it too in fact i know
it practically by heart because my father no
slouch himself as a storyteller has taken great
pleasure in recounting it over the years but you
could also check it out by searching old federal
& state tax rolls & new york city department of
labor employment records & the files of new york
local 65 & other available archives & david would
probably confirm the name of his subject to you
as he did to me when i met him in san diego in
1974 shortly after first reading this piece of his

the poem is called "the london march: an
improvisation for 2 voices" & has become a
famous one at least in certain admittedly small
circles that value a specific narrow approach
to experimental poetry according to marjorie
perloff who should know it is certifiably bluechip
avantgarde & has attained the status of a classic
influencing the language poetry movement perloff
says so i suppose that to whatever extent
artists confer immortality on their subjects a

dicey notion at best very presumptuous to say
the least david thus immortalized my father
though i think pop has other & better claims
to fame in any case my interest here has to do
with exploring the relationship between poetic
license & poetic justice

david produced this work in 1968 first published
it in 1972 & then reissued it in 2001 presumably
performing it publicly along the way so obviously
it has sat well with him & he stands by it the
event he describes in it involving my father
occurred some 10 years previously 1958 hence in
assessing davids account we must make allowances
for the inevitable elisions of memory & also of
course take into consideration poetic license
since david enjoys the privileges that come with
poetic license because hes a poet he says so &
so do quite a few other people

in the passage in question david writes about
a strike in which he was involved "when i was
working for the translating outfit that was
filled with old communists the owner was an old
communist turned capitalist" that was my father
his name is earl coleman & "the translating
outfit" was a publishing house that he & my
mother founded together her name was frances
coleman she died in 2000 the business was called
consultants bureau enterprises incorporated it
had its offices in new york city at 227 west 17th
street in manhattan

now the first thing i want to point out here is
that as everyone who worked for them knew very
well my mother & father were co-owners of &
equal partners in this business with my father
serving as ceo thats chief executive officer
& my mother as eic that stands for editor in
chief simply a division of labor they made all
decisions jointly which means that since david
was employed in a copyediting capacity there
my mother was davids actual boss he would have
been hired by her & would have reported directly
to her not to my father yet david has erased
her my mother frances coleman entirely from his

narrative is that poetic license or fallible
memory or inconvenient truth or sexism & does
it connect in any way to the fact that david in
this book cannot decide on the correct spelling
of his own wifes nickname i cant say

a second fact to get on the record here is that
in 1958 my father earl the "old communist turned
capitalist" was all of 42 & his business partner
my mother frances fran as everyone called her
was all of 43 not exactly "old" except in the
sense of former or ex as in my old girlfriend or
my old school which perhaps is closer to what
david meant to imply david was 26 at the time
thus less than a generation younger than this
"old communist turned capitalist" do we chalk
that up to poetic license or ageism or just
sloppy phrasing beats me

be that as it may the "old communist turned
capitalist" that is to say my father had set
aside his dream of writing poetry & fiction
fulltime in order to keep body & soul together
by creating & running this enterprise with my
mother so possibly having a younger poet in
their employ conspiring behind their backs
on company time to unionize their business
constituted either poetic license or poetic
justice or both you can decide that once youve
heard the story

david goes on to say "the translators were all
old communists" & that was mostly true with the
same caveat regarding the operative definition
of "old" i remind you this was the height of the
cold war & still the mccarthy era & these "old
communists turned capitalist" that is to say the
team of my mother & father had cleverly created
a business that enabled them to hire a bunch
of "old communists" who were otherwise almost
completely unemployable given the repressive
political atmosphere of the time

they were translating top level soviet scientific
journals for the english speaking scientific
community thus keeping that scientific community

all of which basically was funded by the
military industrial complex in this country
closely informed of just how advanced soviet
science was at the time & exactly how close to
if not ahead of american science the soviet
chemists & physicists & biologists were thus
arguably this translation project founded by
these "old communists turned capitalist" helped
to maintain the uneasy balance of power between
the two main contenders during the cold war by
making sure the top echelon of hawkish military
& civilian scientists here knew that they had
no significant exploitable advantage over their
soviet counterparts

my parents the "old communists turned capitalist"
by necessity did business with the ussr openly
& officially in order to obtain the translation
rights to & advance copies of these journals
that enabled this project which made the whole
enterprise politically suspect to the nth degree
from the perspective of the domestic thought
police so while they couldnt have put those
"old communist translators" on the company
payroll on fulltime salary or had them coming in
every day to work in the office without getting
snarled up in all kinds of fbi surveillance &
security checks & other harassing investigations
they could & did outsource as we say today the
translation assignments to those "old communist
translators" on a freelance basis & pay them
well for their efforts thus helping them to
survive in a time of terrible oppression of old
& young communists alike thats capitalism in
action for you

next comes an odd moment in davids poem in which
he starts to describe the strike he says or
writes "the printer was a beautiful grey-haired
leftist older woman from new england she used
to wear blue workshirts & no makeup and she led
a strike against the communist owner" note that
while the woman printer gets featured here my
mother frances coleman the editor in chief of
a major scientific technical publishing house in
the late 1950s certainly an unusual distinction

in fact the only woman in such a position in
the publishing industry at the time still goes
unmentioned in davids tale while my father who
along with mom left the communist party in
the late thirties upon the announcement of the
stalin-hitler pact & various dictates from the
cpusa to the artists & writers in the membership
requiring them to start churning out social
realist agitprop has somehow inexplicably become
"the communist owner" but here comes the really
interesting part so pay close attention

"she led a strike against the communist owner
for demoting gloria actually he promoted her
the negro receptionist because she was so
bitchy and turning all the customers away jane
called out everybody on strike" now you might
well ask how you justify a strike because
someone gets promoted but david chooses not to
explain doubtless more poetic license but i had
worked in the business summers in the shipping
department run by nestor a puerto rican so
i knew gloria who though wellgroomed & smart
had a really nasty manner perpetually snide &
meantempered & brusque

no business can thrive when their public face
at the front desk alienates people & gloria
was unpleasant across the board to messenger
boys nobel prizewinning scientists dignitaries
from washington & even her fellow employees
who had to get buzzed in & out by her through
the vestibule where she was stationed unless
they went around the back to take the freight
elevator or used the stairs which more than a
few did just to avoid her

so after endless complaints from visitors &
clients & her coworkers & trying various gentle
forms of suasion to get gloria to adjust her
attitude & treat people courteously in person
& on the phone my parents gave her a raise
& reassigned her to another division of the
company with a different job description out of
the public eye where she couldnt do that sort of
harm a most humane & reasonable solution to my

way of thinking & perfectly legal too but david obviously believed in 1958 when this took place & in 1968 when he initially created the piece in question & presumably still believed in 2001 when he republished it that this promotion of gloria with pay raise justified a strike because as he somehow neglects to mention david took an active role in planning that strike

by the way when david says "jane called out everybody on strike" hes lying this isnt a matter of poetic license or interpretation or inadvertent elision its demonstrable deliberate falsehood of course the companys owners my parents that is couldnt have reassigned a worker that way in a union shop without going through the shop steward & various hearings regardless of cause that would be definite grounds for a strike in a union shop

so you need to know as david surely knows that "the translating outfit" was not a union shop when this strike took place thus it constituted what is generally known as a "wildcat" strike & jane was not the elected union shop steward although davids phrasing insinuates otherwise which means that jane had no authority to "call out everybody on strike" a call every member of a union shop would have had to obey but as this was a wildcat strike in fact "everybody" did not go out on strike only a handful of employees heeded her call while most stayed on the job not exactly the dramatic waiting for lefty norma rae moment david evokes here

the company wasnt unionized because the employees hadnt found it necessary since the "old communists turned capitalist" who owned it my parents that is always treated their staff very well a few years later the company would go public and theyd choose to institute a profitsharing plan whereby everyone who had worked for the company for a certain number of years got a prorated number of shares plus stock options & would receive more shares plus options proportionally the longer they worked there &

the higher they rose some of them eventually
retired very rich as a result

even before that though by the time of this
wildcat strike in 1958 they hired people of
both genders & all gender persuasions & ages &
ethnicities based strictly on their qualifications
& promoted people on merit alone regardless
of any of that in the fifties they had already
voluntarily initiated what we now call flexitime
to accommodate people who for some reason
couldnt keep normal business hours they gave
paid sick leave & paid maternity leave & paid
vacations & health coverage & annual bonuses &
regular raises & promotions

a few pages further on david mentions nestors
musical group and nestors hope that "they were
going to make it big on the porto rican radio
stations" nestor sang bass and some of the other
shipping clerks were in the group they would
rehearse during lunch hours they liked the
acoustics in the stairwell i recall & sometimes
theyd even break into their repertoire while
on duty in the mailroom but david omits the
fact of which nestor was very proud that my
father and mother the "old communists turned
capitalist" were bankrolling his group they
paid the production costs for the groups first
album and single the single got some airplay
on local stations but never went anywhere &
the group eventually disbanded my parents lost
a few thousand bucks on that venture but didnt
begrudge it they encouraged people there to
think big & follow their dreams something of an
extended family atmosphere prevailed

"old communists" that they were they also
allowed people who were homebound because of
obligations of childcare or eldercare or due
to infirmities to work from home including
typists to whom they would lend these huge
heavy expensive ibm electric typewriters built
like tanks purchased transported installed &
periodically serviced in their own apartments at
company expense so the employees were reasonably

satisfied on the whole on top of which they
represented for that era & even ours an unusual
degree of what nowadays we term diversity
with not only "old communists" but black &
hispanic & asian & gay & lesbian workers at all
levels of the hierarchy as you have probably
guessed by now jane the strike leader with her
blue workshirts & no makeup was a very butch
stalinist i remember her well though i thought
my mother much more beautiful but then i am
prejudiced

so aside from the inevitable office squabbles &
some minimal amount of employee dissatisfaction
well within the range of statistical probability
working conditions were so good at "the
translating outfit" that turnover was unusually
low they were a relatively content & welloff
group of workers with few grievances however
a new york union local 65 with ambitions of
organizing the entire publishing industry
selected this little independent company that
they considered easy pickings to set a precedent
using jane as their stalking horse david served
as her undercover insider ally they sought high
& low for a complaint that would justify a
strike & glorias unsolicited promotion was the
only excuse they could find a flimsy one at best
you might agree some would consider it nothing
more than a pretext

since this was not a union shop & the companys
wildcatting employees hadnt joined up or paid
dues the union couldnt or wouldnt offer them
strike funds in place of lost wages or much
material support of any kind so they didnt get
many employees to join the strike & had to fill
out the picket line with members of the local on
strike at other places or with nothing better to
do

the consultants bureau office was only a few
blocks east of the docks on the hudson piers
so a bunch of these standins were longshoremen
at least thats my best guess i remember seeing
them several times when i went down to the office

during the strike i was in & out of the premises on a regular basis during those years running family errands on top of working there summers so i recognized most of the employees by sight & knew these grizzled musclebound guys had never been part of the crew

some of the few who did walk out had motives other than indignation over glorias promotion or any legitimate labor issue as david himself writes "my partner the guy i used to edit the russian automation journal with was afraid not to go out on strike too even though he hated gloria because his mother was the editor of the last stalinist journal in america and he was afraid jane would tell on him if he crossed the picket lines" now theres a principled position of politically mature workingclass solidarity for you

remember too that these "old communists turned capitalist" earl & fran my parents fran the daughter of a west virginia house painter & carpenter & earl the son of a cutter in the garment district survivors of the depression who together had built this business from the ground up scrabbling for a decade working 16 to 20 hour days & who though extremely selfeducated widely read & articulate had less than three years of college between them were giving gainful 9 to 5 employment with benefits to david who at that point had a mere bachelor of arts degree with undergraduate credits in science & languages from ccny the city college of new york which had pretty much zero value as a professional credential

i earned a bachelors degree from hunter a different college in the same city system a few years later so i know exactly what that diploma was worth on the open market meaning that for david it was either do proofreading scutwork somewhere or teach highschool science or french & instead he got to be involved in the editorial production of the english language edition of a distinguished soviet journal of automation

given the attitude on davids part toward this
opportunity provided to him & toward those
who provided it one can imagine the quality of
davids work & his dedication to it while with
"the translating outfit" one thing my parents
always valued above all else was work hard work
of any kind the sanctity of honest labor mental
or physical the imperative of commitment to ones
work & the necessity of ensuring the quality
thereof they taught that to their employees
by example working harder than anyone there
certainly harder than david did while in their
employ i guarantee you that

it was probably not david who made the
intermittent weekday afternoon calls to our
house that i received during the strike these
calls were carefully timed they came around 4:15
pm when my younger brother dennis or i or both
of us would be home from school but my parents
normally still at work the caller always male
always gruff would give no name but simply say
"your father & mother wont be coming home" or
"dont expect to see your parents again" & hang
up too short a call to trace the police told me
unsettling you might imagine for a 15 year old i
would phone the office to check with my folks to
make sure they were unharmed

when i met david in 1974 & we talked about this
episode i didnt ask if that had been him on the
phone perhaps because i doubted he had whatever
it took to handle that chore though also because
if he had answered yes i would have punched him
in the face but i do assume that as a junior
ringleader of the strike he knew this went on
it was surely approved by the strike committee
& after all nothing more than the usual fifties
union bullyboy thuggery so maybe in his mind a
form of fiction covered by poetic license

though he worked for a company specializing in
translation of scientific journals & had a few
undergraduate science courses under his belt
david did not qualify as a rocket scientist
witness the fact that he left an assortment of

highly sensitive material about the strike from
his secret conferences with jane the printer &
the rest of the strike committee in his unlocked
desk in the company office

my parents being "old communists turned
capitalist" & all that figured that since they
paid davids salary paid the rent on the office &
owned this desk they had a right to look inside
it especially after the strike committee made
an illegal copy of the companys client list
and contacted them all urging each one to stop
doing business with the company thus threatening
the companys very survival and of course the
livelihoods of all those who worked there

so one night after hed clocked out they found
davids notes hence they pretty much knew the
strike committees plans & nose count which gave
them a certain edge of course they never let on
that they had this inside info so if david ever
reads this or jane if shes still alive theyll
learn for the first time that david betrayed his
cause through naivete & indiscretion that would
probably constitute poetic justice

i wonder if david has always done that i mean
when hes pursued any subsequent politicking in
his other occupational environments including
in his eventually tenured teaching position
in the art department at the university of
california san diego where hes now professor
emeritus he landed there in 1968 the same year
he wrote &/or talked this piece has he always
left the evidence of his subrosa dealings in
his office drawers or on the hard drive of his
office computer on the assumption that the people
against whom he has maneuvered would consider
those sacrosanct

when reading this piece of davids which i hope
you will do as a reality check you may find it
odd that after pointedly raising the issue of
this strike david doesnt tell you how it came
out that too perhaps falls under the heading
of poetic license or maybe forgetfulness but

23

the reason could also be that the strike failed
because the full roster of employees of "the
translating outfit" voted by a considerable
majority against unionizing the company that is
to say janes & davids unionization scheme did
not succeed & their presumption of representing
& speaking for their fellow workers was soundly
& publicly repudiated by those very same people

what happened was that from perusing the notes
that david had made available to them my father
& mother knew who the likely supporters of
unionization would be & how many there were
according to the strike committees own tally
which showed the company had a slight edge but
wasnt a sure winner it was standard practice
in such situations that the fulltime employees
minus anyone considered management would have
the opportunity to vote on whether or not they
wanted to have union representation my parents
had considered how to handle this so when it
came time to negotiate the terms of the voting
process my father as company ceo met with jane
the printer as head of the strike committee
along with the representative of the union local
that would control the shop if the pro union
side won

per protocol jane demanded a vote on
unionization & insisted that a date get set for
this then the "old communist turned capitalist"
my father that is inquired "does that mean a
vote by all the employees except for management"
& jane said "of course" & earl said "surely that
doesnt include the translators & the parttimers
& the people who work at home" all of whom he
knew were not on the secret list of likely pro
union ballots that jane & david had drawn up
because they hadnt considered them as potential
voters & jane immediately said "if they work
for the company they vote" because many of
those people were her good friends & also "old
communists" so she was sure she had their votes

well the union delegate her handler gasped &
rolled his eyes knowing as jane did not because

she was no rocket scientist herself that theyd
lost the election right then & there even before
it took place but he couldnt say so or force
jane to retract that commitment once made though
he pulled her aside and tried hard my father
taking no notice of the union reps dismay then
on behalf of the company reluctantly agreed to
the vote on those terms on the indicated date

so jane the greyhaired leftist printer & david
her young line editor collaborator failed to
understand that all the people whom she thereby
authorized to vote would cast their ballots
according to their own economic self interests
thats intro to marxism 101 of course those
who worked for the company fulltime could see
clearly that unionization would immediately end
the flexitime & bonuses & various other benefits
they enjoyed

meanwhile the "old communist translators" &
the other freelancers & the people working
from home could be sure that if the union
took control theyd get cut loose pronto not
by managements choice but at the insistence of
the union itself because unions cant tolerate
freelancers or people working outside the shop &
thus unsupervised by the shop steward they all
knew which side their bread was buttered on that
wasnt rocket science either just dismal science
perhaps youll find poetic justice in there
somewhere

in this way without any overt or covert threats
or strikebreaking tactics or pleading or bribes on
the part of the "old communists turned capitalist"
the unionization campaign at consultants bureau
collapsed with jane & david discredited as
spokespersons for the employees easy enough for
any researcher to document all this i might add &
i suppose david would admit to it if asked though
in this poem which he structured as a dialogue his
chosen interlocutor his wife eleanor or elly or
ely the one with the indeterminate nickname simply
follows his script in which she tactfully refrains
from pressing the point

does this constitute poetic justice in any case
it provides an alternative to poetic license as
the explanation for david offering no denouement
to the episode but instead moving right along to
something else saying only a few pages further on
that he had dated someone named "millie she even
got a job there as a sort of assistant editor"
then "that was later after i left the translating
company" actually he got fired you can understand
that david would pass over those details that dont
portray him in a favorable light hes only human
after all & even if he hadnt been canned it would
have been embarrassing to stay on there after ones
supposedly pro labor initiative got defeated by
actual working people

so david wisely went back to school to get
a masters in linguistics & stayed in school
thereafter just switching from one side of
the schooldesk to the other parlaying that
subsequent nonterminal degree plus all
the hardearned insights from his days as a
grassroots organizer in the labor movement into
an academic sinecure he has managed to build
a considerable reputation for himself as a
poet & art critic & theorist over the ensuing
decades in some small part by fictionalizing &/
or poeticizing &/or falsifying this experience
of his within a business created & run by my
parents earl & frances coleman

when i met david in spring 1974 i had come to
the university of california san diego as a
visiting critic at the invitation of some faculty
in the art department there an art department
in which david & his wife the performance artist
eleanor antin also taught it was a hothouse for
academic marxism i discovered herbert marcuse of
the frankfurt school has found his final refuge
there the faculty whod invited me & their grad
students had even formed a little cell that
huddled in the evenings as a study group it had
a definite timewarp quality to it something akin
to a sanctuary for endangered species & struck
a melancholy vaguely nostalgic note for someone
like myself who had grown up around members of

the old left & gone to school with some of the
new left wannabes of the late fifties & early
sixties whom i instinctively avoided like the
plague

i recall that one of those grads who has since
gone on to a thriving career as an academic
artist & theorist had attempted a translation
of a roland barthes essay on semiotics &
photography unfortunately he didnt know french
so the translation which consisted of word
substitutions taken straight from a french-
english dictionary was shall we say spotty
mostly fragmentary phrases inaccurately &
unidiomatically rendered none of the rest of
them spoke or read french either i watched them
sit around all evening scratching their heads
trying to figure out what this stuff meant like
hapless scholars reverently handing the dead sea
scrolls around before they found the key

i could tell his translation was severely off
because i am bilingual francophone the result
of two years in a public school in the south of
france in the early 1950s when my parents "the
old communists turned capitalist" hounded by
the fbi expatriated to europe a most powerful
experience of exile internalized by me as such
though not fully understood for many years so i
could look at the barthes original & see this
students copious & grave mistakes in translation
but didnt have the heart to humiliate him by
pointing these out in front of his classmates &
faculty

i assumed i had been invited to ucsd in the
expectation or hope that i would approve this
indoctrinational daisychain enterprise & give
them all or at least some that i handpicked
from the lot my blessing & then provide career
boosts to the anointed few in other words
typical artschool jockeying for favors from
influential visitors but thats not the way i
work so i decided just to stay out of their way
from then on & not interfere with their project
which even though they have mostly done very

well for themselves indeed apparently came as a
big disappointment to them i learned that years
later from the former girlfriend of one of the
faculty members who was briefly my lover in new
york

this grad student who had attempted the
barthes translation was already larding his
pronouncements with the telling phrase "as we
all know" one of the signature tropes of the
totalitarian mind a semantically manipulative
device for the rhetorical creation of spurious
consensus i have had the opportunity to watch
him lecture publicly & teach classes since
& have read his writings & that phrase has
become a verbal tic in his locutions but whats
really important about him in relation to this
narrative is that during my first afternoon
on campus he pressed upon me a photocopy of
davids piece the one under consideration here
the one in which my father shows up as "the old
communist turned capitalist" handing this to me
without comment except to indicate that i would
definitely meet david during my stay & should get
to know his work

this grad student & his faculty & his fellow
students were all very tight with david & elly
davids variously spelled wife so i quickly
realized when i first read "the london march"
& recognized therein my parents & this strike
episode that they had discovered this poem was
about my parents & their company perhaps david
had seen my name on the list of forthcoming
visiting critics & made the connection for them
i gathered that theyd planned to drop this on
me as a bombshell hoping perhaps to provoke a
faceoff between david & myself they battened
on that sort of carefully engineered surprise
confrontation as i learned from observing them
over the years thereafter

but while i confirmed with david privately that
this passage did indeed involve my family &
his employment in "the translating outfit" my
parents ran i decided not to take it further

at least not at that time & didnt rise to this
bait i hadnt come to ucsd to engage in some
pissing contest with the antins & didnt want
that distracting from what i intended to present
to the students & faculty for whom i suppose it
thus became the other shoe that never dropped

so i let it slide then & thereafter until i came
across the reissue of davids "talking" at strand
books in manhattan in november 2006 & understood
that for better or worse & not by our own
choosing my family history had entered into the
dna of experimental poetry in the second half
of the twentieth century & decided that we that
is to say us my family who also lived through
that strike to be specific earl & fran & me & my
younger brother dennis that our dna to whatever
extent i embody & represent it should have some
voice in the process

now one question that all this raises at least
in my mind is that if depending on how you view
it david has fictionalized &/or poeticized
&/or falsified the facts of this episode for his
own ulterior motives creative or ideological
or selfserving or manipulative or deceitful or
whatever we take those to be & if this short
passage from this one piece of his occupies only
2 pages total in a piece 60 pages long in a book
of 190 pages merely one of his numerous books
i might add then just how much time & effort
would it take to sort out fact from fiction &
truth from untruth & honesty from duplicity in
40 years worth of davids writings & how much
poetic license do you grant to any poet even
one bearing the imprimaturs of marjorie perloff
& charles bernstein & ron silliman & jerome
rothenberg & robert creeley & sundry others

i cant answer that surely not with any authority
that youd find persuasive because although i
have an established reputation as a photo &
art critic & historian & write & publish poetry
myself no one of any note has confirmed that i
am either a poet or a qualified literary critic
& though my father earl has written & published

much more poetry than i having come back to that
after retiring from his long life as a publisher
he hasnt been validated as an important poet
on the same level as david antin by those whom
david himself would probably call the recognized
poetry "relators" so davids poetic license
outranks my fathers & my own & probably both of
ours combined nonetheless i hope that i have
raised some useful questions here about poetic
license & done at least one poet some poetic
justice

Email Exchange with Charles Bernstein

Subject: Antin piece
From: A. D. Coleman
Date: Tue, 20 May 2014

To: Charles Bernstein

Dear Charles: Good to meet you last night at Bobbie Rosenthal's dinner party, and put a face to the name after all these years.

Per your request, I've attached a PDF file of the David Antin piece we discussed briefly. I've performed it live, but have yet to find a home for it in print. You'll find more about my father and his work at http://stubbornpine.com. Also in the interview at the end of his side of our two-fer book.

Best,

Allan

Subject: Fwd: Antin piece
From: Charles Bernstein
Date: May 21, 2014
To: A. D. Coleman

Dear Allan,

I enjoyed meeting you and talking the other night. Thanks for *Like Father / Like Son,* which I found interesting and the two interviews are informative.

I read te Antin piece with interest and indeed enjoyment though I think the final effect is rather the opposite of what you have in mind. And as I mentioned, I strongly recommend you take a look at Eleanor Antin's Letters for Stalin, which is funny and sad and deals with much of the same social reality that you bring forth in your piece.

I think your focus on two key phrases is telling. One the fact that David refers to his Eleanor with differently spelled nicknames, which I have always liked. The other is the phrase you repeat over and again "old communists turned capitalists."

You take certain I would say inevitable slippages in Antin's poem (which is the explicit subject of much of his work) as a sign of deceit, but your piece overall suggests a monovalent understanding of the facts (as if spelling a name the same way is a virtue) that I find more troubling than whatever you criticize Antin for. And in the end your own presentation of the story here lends itself to a more negative reading of your own account than Antin's -- that is, as a biased reader and friend of David's that I am, I found your sins of misinterpretation and distortion more blatant than anything you quote from David -- and I base this not on a knowledge of the "facts" but just reading your piece. But this is also what I like about the piece -- your passionate defense of your parents and your reliving the inevitable conflicts on the Cold War and the anti-Communist and anti-union hysteria of the time.

My father was always a capitalist and he ran a union shop -- ILGWU, as he had to. When Antin says "old communists turned capitalists" the only sense I ascribe to that is the one you acknowledge -- old meaning "former" NOT old meaning old in age. Your sense that this line is troubling or misleading troubles your piece against the grain of your explicit narrative, since you state that as a matter of fact they were ex-Communists (not a negative category). Another small detail: you suggest that it is deceptive to call a walkout for unionization by some workers at company as a "strike" -- only unions can call strikes and you say Antin should have called this a "wildcat strike": but there is nothing at all deceptive in an anecdote like Antin's to use "strike" in this way and this is a perfectly accurate word for the situation that you describe; what's problematic is your criticism of Antin for saying "strike" rather than your preferred wording "wildcat strike."

For me the decisive turning point in the piece is the "veiled" accusation that Antin was a party to threatening phone calls to your home. Nothing you say supports that: he must have known, you say, but since you note your family obtained the strike plans from his desk and you don't say that this was in the plan, you make clear you have no proof of his involvement. It would be just as easy to assume that some of the non-workers supporting the strike would have done that on their own, given the way you describe them. You seem comfortable with your own insinuations but harsh about the insinuations you attribute to Antin.

Your account of the strike is overshadowed by your apparent distrust of unionizing efforts -- at least for places that might not "need" unions; and your description of union organizers or supporters as the moral equivalent of "scabs." It is horrendous that you were threatened -- but as you know such threats took place on both sides of the divide and the preponderance of such thuggery was anti-union. As memoir, it is of course the injury to you and your parents you recall; but to me as a later reader, your account has the scent of, well, ex-communists turned anti-communists and anti-union.

Your criticism of Antin in this piece -- which strikes me as failing to land a blow -- does come back to haunt you as you seem more guilty of what you accuse of Antin of than anything you say about him. I would chalk it up to poetic license and the perils of memoir -- but it's your own aversion to "poetic license" that makes the many such licenses you take stand out. I find this very contradiction interesting about what you write.

I wish you realized how odd it is to say this anecdote about your parent's business had some effect on Antin's career -- but then your piece is woven with a kind of belittling of not only Antin's art but also of those who regarded it highly, as if all this is somehow tainted by a failure to be truthful, based on tricks: that just adds to what I find the anti-communist anti-modernist anti-union intimations in what you write here. What starts as a memoir ends up as a piece of ideological contest that wants to deny its own ideological position. Eg: because your parents worked hard and treated workers well is not a reason to be against unions or even a union at their business; that workers often voted against unionization does not mean that unionization does not have social and economic value for workers; the fact that non-working class people support unions does not make them hypocritical; the fact that an artist (like me) has tenure does not mean this is -- as you say of Antin's work -- a "sinecure" (which is another telling comment of yours, as if the only people who work hard and deserve respect are you, your parents, and their loyal employees). The "sinecure" charge is exactly what those on the right use -- those who would eliminate tenure and move more university teachers and scholars to adjunct status (similar to the part-timers at your parent's company). For those of us in universities tenure is closely related to union and civil service job protection and also the protection of free speech and many of us support unionization especially if it would cut down on part-timers.

I apologize if I am responding more than you wanted. But since you asked ....

Charles

Subject: Our correspondence re my Antin piece
From: A. D. Coleman
Date: Tue, 29 July 2014

To: Charles Bernstein

Dear Charles:

I appreciate your detailed response to "poetic license/poetic justice."

At the time those events took place [1958] there wasn't yet anything called the "new left." Still, as I suspect you're aware, calling someone an "old communist" in 1968 had connotations that went beyond either "ex-communist" or "former communist." Furthermore, since David goes on to say that "the translators were all old communists," he surely doesn't mean that they were all ex- or former communists, since some of them were still communists, albeit low-profile then for obvious reasons.

Of course there's more to the story. Neither Earl nor Fran ever made a rightward turn toward what you call "anti-communism." Nor did they become in any generalized way anti-union. Unionization would simply have made it impossible for them to continue their project, dependent as it was on rare specialists who had serious chops in both science and Russian translation, yet whose full-time employment would have been impossible for political reasons. The pro-unionization clique, including David, didn't care about that -- or didn't understand it.

I don't fault David for not calling that situation a "wildcat strike." I fault him for implying that "Jane" was a shop steward empowered to "call everyone out on strike," and for implying that this is what happened -- absolutely false in every particular. I fault him for endorsing a strike based on an incomprehensible "grievance" -- the promotion of a black employee -- and for failing to enunciate clearly his own motives for joining the pro-union faction, given that he demonstrably doesn't take seriously this "grievance" of Gloria's promotion and articulates no causal grievances of his own. I fault him for eliding the outcome of the situation, which -- both the outcome and the elision -- does not reflect well on him. I find all of that smug and self-serving, a quality that runs through much of the work of his that I've absorbed (not his complete oeuvre, by any means, just a relative sampling thereof).

Most of all, I fault him for his casually dismissive attitude toward my parents and the business they spent much of their life building, a business that I believe made positive contributions (from a left-wing standpoint) on many levels during a very fraught time. And I fault him for his complete erasure of his direct superior, my mother, the company's EIC, from his narrative. That offends me. So, on that basis, I've exercised the Rashomon option here, adding another version of the tale. No doubt this will offend some, and open me up to similar scrutiny by others, yourself included, which I find perfectly appropriate -- poetic justice, in fact.

I'm not anti-union, though I disapprove of some unionizing tactics just as much as I do some strike-breaking tactics. I turned down a full-time job offer from the *NY Times* that would have gotten me into the Newspaper Guild (but not for that reason). I'm a founding member of the National Writers Union (not a real union, I hasten to add, despite its affiliation with the UAW). I turned down two tenure-track teaching offers (though not for that reason); but, though I think it needs revamping, I believe in the tenure system, even if I don't benefit from it directly.

My politics aren't my parents', but then I have the benefit of hindsight. However you'd classify me, based on the positions I've articulated over the years, I doubt that you'd have an easy time persuading anyone that I'm right-wing. So, as ever, I'll take my chances on how others respond to what I have to say.

Thanks for taking the time to spell out your own response so carefully.

Best,

Allan

Charles Bernstein is the author of *Near/Miss* (University of Chicago, 2018), *Pitch of Poetry* (Chicago, 2016), and *Recalculating* (Chicago, 2013). He is Donald T. Regan Professor of English and Comparative Literature at the University of Pennsylvania. His book-length *A Conversation with David Antin*, published by Granary Books in 2002, is available for free download at https://jacket2.org/commentary/antin-bernstein-pdf. More info at writing.upenn.edu/epc.

Frances Allan Coleman
(1915-2000)

Frances Allan Coleman, 85, co-founder and former editor-in-chief of the Plenum Publishing Corporation, died peacefully of natural causes on Saturday, November 4, 2000 in Willits, California. Beginning in the late 1970s Ms. Coleman suffered numerous strokes, and in her last years was diagnosed as an Alzheimer's victim.

Ms. Coleman, the former Frances Louise Allan, was born in Elkins, West Virginia, June 6, 1915, to James and Emily Allan. After a year at Davis & Elkins College she left West Virginia, living briefly in Pittsburgh — where she edited a union newspaper — before moving to New York City.

In New York she worked as an assistant to the noted documentary photographer and filmmaker Arnold Eagle, as a result of which she became a serious amateur photographer, and also found employment as a freelance editor. During World War II she met and married Earl Maxwell Coleman, then a writer of poetry and fiction.

In 1947 they founded a custom translation service,

Consultants Bureau, which they developed into the Plenum Publishing Corporation, a major New York-based scientific-technical publishing house. Consultants Bureau in 1949 pioneered the rapid, efficient, and accurate translation into English of top-level Soviet scientific material in both journal and book form. In 1960, as Consultants Bureau Enterprises, Inc., the company became a publicly held corporation traded on NASDAQ; in 1965, it changed its name to Plenum Publishing Corporation.

By 1965 the company was publishing more than 100 Russian scientific journals in translation — the largest such program in the world — along with numerous English-language scientific journals, as well as 300 new scientific books annually and extensive reprints in the humanities through Da Capo Press, one of its divisions. Ms. Coleman served as editor-in-chief of the entire scientific program of Consultants Bureau and then Plenum Publishing from its beginnings until 1965, when she retired.

Her marriage to Earl M. Coleman ended in divorce in 1965. Upon leaving Plenum, Ms. Coleman traveled widely: in south and central America, in Finland, and in Africa. She reactivated her earlier interest in photography, relocating for several years to San Francisco, where she took courses at the San Francisco Art Institute with Ralph Gibson and Larry Clark. She soon began exhibiting and publishing her pictures under the pen name Fran Allan, eventually specializing in wildlife photography. Her work, represented by the agencies Black Star and Animals Animals, appeared in print internationally.

In 1977 she returned from a lengthy stay in Kenya and co-purchased the Wagon Wheel Ranch in Willits, California, in Mendocino County, which she shared with her life partner, the Canadian John Hatch, until his death from lung cancer in 1990. She continued to live on her ranch, with full-time private care, and died at home.

Earl Maxwell Coleman
(1916-2009)

Earl Maxwell Coleman, 93, co-founder and former publisher of the Plenum Publishing Corporation, died of a pulmonary embolism on Monday, October 12, 2009. He lived in Somerset, N.J.

Mr. Coleman was born in the Bronx, New York City, New York, January 9, 1916, to Samuel and Rose Cohen. Mrs. Cohen subsequently changed the family name to Coleman. After a year at the City College of New York Mr. Coleman enlisted in the U.S. Air Force, where he became a Link Trainer instructor. He served in the U.S., England, and Ireland until the war's end.

During World War II Coleman met and married Frances Louise Allan, then a freelance editor and a serious amateur photographer. Upon returning to the States he pursued a career as a writer of fiction and poetry, represented by the noted left-wing literary agent Max Lieber. Despite some early success, including publication of a short story in *Esquire*, he felt unsure of his ability to earn a living as a writer. Mr. and Mrs. Coleman founded a custom translation service, Consultants Bureau, in 1947. Two years later, as the Cold War intensified, Consultants Bureau pioneered the rapid, efficient, and accurate translation into English of top-level Soviet scientific material in both journal and book form. In 1960, as Consultants Bureau Enterprises, Inc., the company became a publicly held corporation traded on NASDAQ.

Consultants Bureau Enterprises changed its name to Plenum Publishing Corporation in 1965. By that time it had become a major New York-based scientific-technical publishing house. The company was then producing more than 100 Russian scientific journals in translation — the largest such program in the world — along with numerous English-language scientific journals, as well as 300 new scientific books annually. Additionally, Plenum issued extensive reprints in the humanities through Da Capo Press, one of its divisions, founded in 1963. Mr. Coleman served as publisher of Consultants Bureau and then Plenum Publishing from its beginnings until he sold his interest in that company in 1977. In 1996 Wolters Kluwer purchased Plenum Publishing for US$258m.

Mr. Coleman's marriage to Frances Coleman ended in divorce in 1965. Upon leaving Plenum, Mr. Coleman began a new publishing venture, with his second wife Ellen Schneid Coleman as editor-in-chief. This imprint specialized in edited collections of notable public-domain material, such as the collected presidential speeches of Richard M. Nixon.

In 1984 Mr. Coleman became executive publisher of National Publishers of the Black Hills, the textbook division of a national chain of technical-vocational schools. In tandem with his wife Ellen, who became that imprint's editor-in-chief, he transformed this line from a money-losing project to a successful publishing operation. In 1988 this line of books and its imprint were acquired by Prentice Hall. Mr. Coleman served briefly as a consultant to the imprint's new owners, his last professional role in the publishing world.

All through his decades of activity as a publisher Mr. Coleman had continued to write poetry and short fiction intermittently. At the conclusion of his business career he returned to creative writing, pursuing it passionately and full-time. Between 1982 and 2009 he published more than 300 lyric poems in print and online literary journals, many of them collected in three books, including *Stubborn Pine in a Stiff Wind* (Mellen Poetry Press, 2001) and *Like Father Like Son* (Villa Florentine Press, 2007), a collaboration with his eldest son Allan.

During that same period he published some 50 short stories; two of them earned him nominations for the prestigious Pushcart Prize in 1999 and 2003. He also completed an unpublished novel and a memoir of the first three decades of his life. At the time of his death he was revising his first foray into theater, a three-act play set in the late 1950s, and working on an assortment of poems and short stories. A selection of his work appears online at his website, Stubborn Pine (stubbornpine.com).

In 1992, while living with his wife in Greenburgh, New York, Mr. Coleman — who had run writers' workshops for adults in the 1940s and early 1950s — initiated an extracurricular writers' workshop for young people aged 8-16, sponsored by the Arts and Culture Committee of Greenburgh. Many of his students went on to publish in adult literary magazines, some while still in his classes. After moving to Somerset, NJ, he continued to commute to teach this workshop until a week before his death.

Mr. Coleman is survived by his wife, Ellen Coleman; his two sons, Allan Douglass Coleman, a writer and teacher in New York City, and Dennis Scott Coleman, a real-estate broker in Garrett Park, MD; his daughter-in-law, Allan Coleman's wife, Anna Chi Hung Lung; his four grandchildren: Edward Allan Coleman, a chef in New York City, Allison Taylor Coleman, a social worker, Max Wellington Coleman, a college student, and Jacky Siu Lung Choi; and his sister, Lucille Bandes, a retired librarian, and brother-in-law, Seymour Bandes, a retired printer.

Afterword & Acknowledgements

Engaging as it does with events now dating back more than half a century, this text, written in 2006 in an approximation of the style of David Antin's "talking poems," assumes that anyone who takes the trouble to read it will bring to it some knowledge of the politics of the era, some awareness of the poetry scene from that period till now, and some interest in both. With those as givens, it aspires to provide all the information necessary to understand the issues at play. For that reason I present it here without prefatory explanation, hoping the reader will elect to plunge in and wade through.

At the same time, questions inevitably get raised therein that the piece itself doesn't answer. And of course it's one-sided, a counter-narrative to the version of those events that provoked it.

To enrich it further, then, and to challenge my own perspective on these matters, I asked poet and critic Charles Bernstein — who has published extensively on David Antin's work — for permission to append thereto an email exchange between us about this piece that took place in the spring of 2014. He graciously agreed, for which I thank him.

I have also included the obituaries I wrote and sent to the *New York Times* upon my parents' deaths. The *Times* did not acknowledge my mother's passing, but used my draft of my father's obit as the basis for their report of his death. I wrote these in as neutral a tone as I could muster on those occasions, merely stating central facts about their lives, for the record. I hope that these summaries will serve as background, enabling the reader to construct more detailed versions of Earl and Frances as protagonists in this drama.

Extensive biographical information on and critical response to the work of David Antin (1932-2016) appears online.

•

For younger readers, and for older ones who may need reminders, a bit of additional context: By 1958, when the wildcat strike at the center of these narratives took place, most unions in this country had energetically and enthusiastically purged from their ranks, or at least silenced the voices of, anyone vocally to the left of the Democratic Party. Thus the very people on whom my parents' enterprise relied would have been barred from union membership due to their past (and in some cases still current) political affiliations.

Moreover, rather than recruiting members from minority populations (e.g., people of color, "out" LGBTQ people), unions in 1958 actively kept such membership at a minimum. Just a few years later the leaders and the rank and file would become proudly right-wing flag-waving patriots, delighting in violently attacking their fellow citizens protesting the war in Vietnam and other domestic and international problems. Paradoxically, perhaps attributable in part to the unionization of police forces nationwide, the unions in this country also made common cause with officers of the law in repressing students and others involved in what we at the left end of the spectrum then broadly called "the movement."

In 1968, when Antin recorded his "london march," union involvement with organized crime in the U.S. was at an all-time high. This partnership "thrived practically unopposed" until the mid-1970s, according to James Jacobs of the New York University School of Law. Homophobia was rampant among the membership, and anti-intellectualism pervaded union culture. Union members were also at the forefront of white flight to the suburbs, helping to devastate the inner cities of the U.S. Moreover, as Edmund F. Wehrle points out in *Between a River and a Mountain: The AFL-CIO and the Vietnam War* (Ann Arbor: University of Michigan Press, 2005), with its unequivocal support of the disastrous Vietnam War "the AFL-CIO helped shape the contours of U.S. involvement in Vietnam — and the war in turn reshaped the American labor movement."

So an uncritically pro-union posture was problematic in 1958, the year of the failed strike at Consultants Bureau that Antin talks about, as it was in 1968 (the year he produced that "talking poem"), when many union members across the country happily beat up left-wingers in public and helped to elect the subsequently disgraced Richard Nixon on a "law and order" platform, following that with the infamous "Hard Hat Riot" of 1970. And an uncritically pro-union posture remains problematic today, however much one respects and endorses the right of labor to bargain collectively in its own interest.

I would direct any reader interested in my nuanced relationship to modernism in the arts to my critical writings on photography and related matters, which I have published since 1968 under the byline A. D. Coleman. To pursue that further, visit my blog, *Photocritic International* (photocritic.com).

•

All citations herein come from David Antin, *Talking* (Normal, IL: Dalkey Archive Press, 2001; first edition, New York: Kulchur Foundation, 1972). In the latest edition this piece appears on pp. 83-142.

The quote from Robert Creeley that opens this piece appears as a blurb on the back of the jacket of Antin's book *i never knew what time it was* (Berkeley: Univ. of California Press, 2005).

The main text of this piece replicates the published style of the Antin piece to which it responds. Hence the lower case, absence of punctuation, etc. In the Antin text, paragraphs (or sections of the prose/poetry) are separated by spaces, as mirrored in this text.

•

Finally, my thanks to Barbara Rosenthal of Washington Street Press, whose enthusiasm for this project and design skills have made its publication possible.

— A. D. C.

About the Author

Born in Brooklyn, New York, on December 19, 1943, a writer since his adolescence, from a family of writers, Allan Douglass Coleman did his undergraduate work in English Literature at Hunter College (Bronx, New York). He received his M.A. in 1967 from the Creative Writing Program at San Francisco State College.

Shortly after earning that degree Coleman returned to New York City and began working professionally as a freelance cultural journalist under the pen name A. D. Coleman, specializing in writing about contemporary photography and the new digital technologies. He has since published 8 books and more than 2500 essays on photography and related subjects. Formerly a columnist for the *Village Voice*, the *New York Times*, and the New York Observer, Coleman has contributed to *Artforum, ARTnews, Technology Review, Juliet Art Magazine* (Italy), *European Photography* (Germany), *La Fotografia* (Spain), and *Art Today* (China), among others. His work has been translated into 21 languages and published in 31 countries.

In 2002 Coleman received the Culture Prize of the German Photographic Society. In 2010 he received the J Dudley Johnston Award from the Royal Photographic Society (U.K.) for "sustained excellence in writing about photography." In 2014 he received the Society for Photographic Education's Insight Award for lifetime contribution to the field, and in 2015 the Society of Professional Journalists SDX Award for Research About Journalism.

Coleman's blog, *Photocritic International,* appears at photocritic.com. Since 2005, exhibitions that he has curated have opened at museums, galleries, and festivals in Canada, China, Finland, Hong Kong, Italy, Rumania, Slovakia, Spain, Taiwan, and the U.S.

Returning to creative writing in the late 1980s, Coleman has since published poetry, short fiction, and creative nonfiction in such journals as *Assembling, BlackWater Review, California Quarterly, The Cape Rock, The Chaffin Journal, Creative Nonfiction, Cross Currents, Defined Providence, Et cetera, Ginosko Literary Journal, Home Planet News, International Poetry Review, Koja, Lalitamba, Nimrod, Passager, Peilikuva* (Finland), *Poem, Poets & Writers, Red Hawk Review, Sanskrit, Talking River Review, Texas Review,* and *The 13th Warrior.*

Coleman's artist's books include *Carbon Copy* (1973), a series of self-portraits, and *Confirmation* (1975), an account of a 1962 pilgrimage to the grave of saxophonist and composer Charles Parker, Jr. In 2000 he released his first book of prose poetry and free verse, *spine,* a collaboration with the Finnish photographer Nina Sederholm. An installation version of that project traveled widely in the Nordic countries. In 2007 he published his second book of prose poetry and free verse, *Like Father Like Son,* shared with his father, Earl M. Coleman, which resulted in his nomination for a Pushcart Prize.

Since the mid-1990s Coleman has read solo and with James Ragan, Joyce Carol Oates, Edmund Keeley, Daniel Halpern, and others, in such locales as Tucson, San Antonio, Las Vegas, Tulsa, and Prague. He has taught creative-writing workshops at the Penland School of Crafts, NC; the Oklahoma Arts Institute; the University of Tulsa; and elsewhere.

Further information about his creative writing appears online at villaflorentine.us.

About the Press

WASHINGTON STREET PRESS is the text-based of the two imprints published by eMediaLoft.org. The other, **x a n a d u   p r e s s**, produces books in which pictures and texts are imaginative, and visually linked. Both are edited by media and performance artist and writer Barbara Rosenthal. Her monthly column of philosophy about the interconnection of art and artist, *A Crack in the Sidewalk*, appears in *Ragazine,* and her bookworks are in the collections of The Whitney, MoMA, Tate, Berlin Kunstbibliotek, Art, et al. No submissions are accepted; publication is by invitation only.

eMediaLoft.org is located within the neon-filled live-work loft Rosenthal shares with Director Emeritus, Bill Creston, within the Westbeth Arts Complex on the Hudson River in the Highline / West Village area of NYC. It is a privately funded loose consortium of artists and others who create hard-to-place, hard-to-categorize works, primarily overlapping within replicable or recordable media: camera and electronic arts, performance and writing, with a strong conceptual base and discernible philosophical perspective.

www.ingramcontent.com/pod-product-compliance
Lightning Source LLC
Chambersburg PA
CBHW050450010526
44118CB00013B/1760